Dino at the

Story by Dianne Irving
Photography by Lindsay Edwards

Rigby®
A Harcourt Achieve Imprint

www.Rigby.com
1-800-531-5015

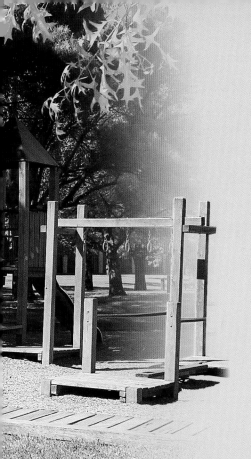

Bella and Karl
went to the park
with Mom.

Dino went, too.

"You can stay down here, Dino,"
said Karl.
"I am going to play
on the swings."

Bella and Karl
went up and down
on the swings.

"Come and play
on the big slide, Karl,"
said Bella.

Karl and Bella
went down the big slide.

"I like this slide," said Karl.

"Bella! Karl!" said Mom.
"We are going home."

Bella and Karl ran to the car.

"Where is Dino?" cried Karl.

"We will help you look for Dino," said Bella.

She ran to look on the slide.

Mom and Karl went to look
on the swings.

"Dino is not here," said Mom.

"Oh!" said Karl.
"He is in the sandbox."

"Dino is hiding down here
in the sand," said Karl.